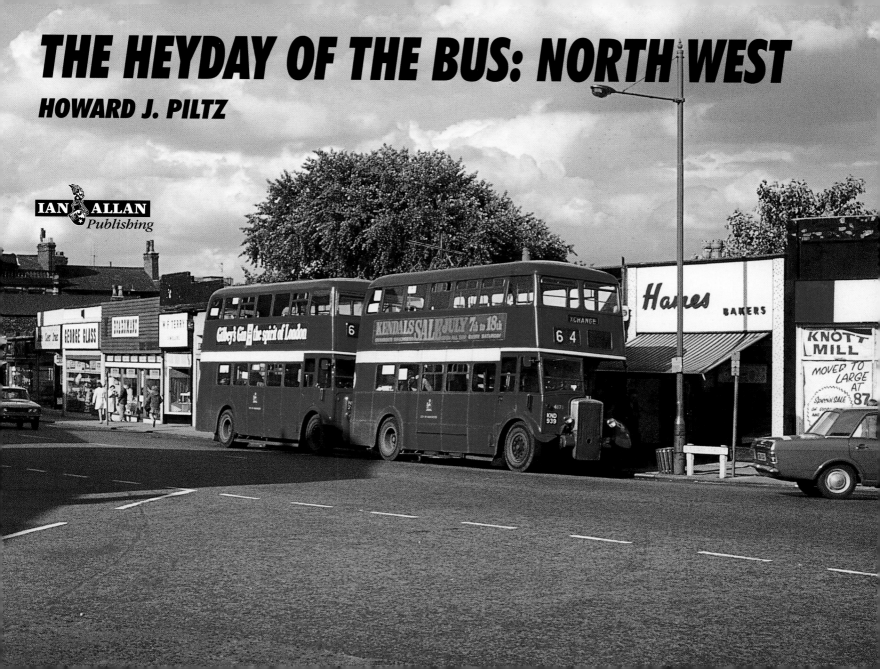

THE HEYDAY OF THE BUS: NORTH WEST

HOWARD J. PILTZ

IAN ALLAN
Publishing

Acknowledgements

As with every book, no one person can be responsible for it in its entirety, and I am happy to thank and acknowledge the assistance of Geoff Lumb, for his encyclopaedic knowledge and veritable Aladdin's cave of reference books and slides; Rob Wilson of Bootle for his knowledge of the Liverpool area and a few gems of transparencies, the origin of which he knows not; fellow Charterplan employee, John Burgoyne, for allowing me to rummage through his collection of early photos, as well as his encouragement to carry out the project; and by no means least — it dare not be! — my beloved wife Christine, for all the washing-up not done.

Title page: The scene at The Downs, Altrincham has barely changed from the days when Manchester's trams would reverse in the middle of the road, right up until the present day, save that if one stood in the middle of the road today to get this shot one would undoubtedly not live to tell the tale! In this view No 4178 is about to do a complete U-turn in order to take up its duty on what continues today as the 263/4 group of services back to the city centre. It is a Daimler CVG6 fitted with Metro Cammell's 'Phoenix' design of body with very few concessions to Manchester's preferences, and that showed a very strong family resemblance to the large fleets of contemporary bodies at Salford, Birmingham, Edinburgh and elsewhere. *Howard J. Piltz*

Front cover: Epitomising the theme of this book, a line-up of affectionately remembered Blackpool Corporation Titans lend a backdrop to a brash, new age depicted here by a brand-new Manchester Corporation Leyland Panther Cub. Inevitably, reminders of our holidays will be rose-tinted and so it is for Blackpool's early postwar Burlingham-bodied Leyland PD2s with their purely ornamental full-fronts and quite impractical centre entrances — but so what! How incongruous seems the visiting saloon, as it transpired, too modernistic for its own good and destined for an uneconomically short life. *Howard J. Piltz*

Back cover: Back to where the tour began, and three Chester Corporation Guy Arabs bask in summer sunshine under possibly Chester's most photographed sight, the Eastgate arch — part of the city's medieval wall. *Howard J. Piltz*

First published 1996

ISBN 0 7110 2460 X

All rights reserved. No part of this book may be reproduced or transmitted in any form or by any means, electronic or mechanical, including photocopying, recording or by any information storage and retrieval system, without permission from the Publisher in writing.

© Ian Allan Ltd 1996

Published by Ian Allan Publishing

an imprint of Ian Allan Ltd, Terminal House, Station Approach, Shepperton, Surrey TW17 8AS.
Printed by Ian Allan Printing Ltd, Coombelands House, Coombelands Lane, Addlestone, Surrey KT15 1HY.

Introduction

Welcome to my imaginary tour of the northwest of England during what for me was its heyday, that time from World War 2, through the 1950s, 1960s and into the early 1970. Life was starting to return to normal after the privations of war and legislation as it affected public transport was still predominantly seen as the furtherance of a service. We are going to look at a region dominated by its two principal cities — Liverpool and Manchester — where, whether it be in business and commerce or the leisure industry of the area, it is impossible to escape the influence of these two great metropolitan areas.

In two respects the buses of the northwest of England were quite distinct. Firstly, such a large proportion of urban services were provided by municipally-owned operators, varying in size from the mega-carriers of the two dominant cities already mentioned to others like Haslingden and Ramsbottom that really were very small undertakings indeed, and it was this richness and diversity of forms, hues and sizes that made the region fascination for the bus enthusiast. Secondly, the density of the inter-working by these operators was unusual. Remember, in the period we are talking about, it was a matter of civic pride that new buses, or trams before them, were added to the fleet as demand grew or earlier machines reached the end of their working lives, and that they were maintained in an immaculate condition. Questions would be asked at the highest level if anything other than the latest machine with the newest paintwork travelled into a neighbouring town; and they *never* left the depot with a dented panel! Listen to Ian Yearsley in his book *The Manchester Tram** recounting the journey of a cheeky Stockport Corporation open-balcony tram of vintage appearance that worked into Manchester on the latter's final day of tramway operation. Sadly, how things have changed.

Interspersed with these municipalities were three operators belonging to the two large nationwide organisations. First of these was the British Electric Traction group, to this day still better known as BET, which was represented by Ribble and North Western, whilst the nationalised 'Tilling' organisation was a grouping of highly standardised companies owned by the British Transport Commission, later to become the Transport Holding Company (THC), and in our region represented by Crosville. These companies provided a wide diversity of services, especially outside the municipalities' operating areas, and tended to be longer-distance.

After World War 2, the region's public transport operators had to cope with the tremendous pent-up demand of a car-less population with a run-down fleet of trams, trolleybuses and motorbuses, many quite definitely on their last legs. Apart from the ever-present fleet in Blackpool, trams were gradually replaced until the region's last ran in Stockport in 1951. Then, as the demands on bus builders to shoulder their share of the responsibility to export for our war-torn economy began to diminish, so new buses could join the hard-pressed bus operators, but as they began to find their feet again, Joe Public discovered the car, and didn't give the bus operating industry a second glance. Inflation was growing as well (I have to confess to remembering — just — a ha'penny fare, roughly a fifth of today's penny to you, son!), and so the spiral of rising fares and fewer passengers began its inexorable progress. The dilemma became a malaise best described by the incident I saw in the mid-sixties when, as a 1947 Manchester Corporation Brush-bodied Daimler passed me on Cheetham Hill Road, it shed a headlight that promptly exploded into a thousand little pieces of glass and metal on the road. Whether or not the driver knew anything of this incident I know not, but the bus carried on, apparently none the worse for its loss.

The redoubtable Barbara Castle was Transport Minister for the Labour government of the day and it was on to her able shoulders that the problem was loaded. As a result, the 1968 Transport Act was designed to produce a two-tiered road transport operation under public control. It formalised the nationalisation of the large BET operation, bringing it under the same overall control as its Tilling contemporaries, that of the Transport Holding Company, for whom the author worked at the time at Argosy House, at the top of Great Portland Street in London's West End. I well remember seeing the payment pass through the system, and what a cheque that was!

Of greater influence on our region was the foundation of the Passenger Transport Executives (PTEs) to co-ordinate and take overall control of bus operations in each of the designated areas. In the fullness of time, it would bring within the control of local or national government virtually all stage carriage operation in these metropolitan areas, save for the odd individual and enigmatic operator that somehow always survives, such as Maynes in east Manchester. The most visible effect was the amalgamation of the municipalities in the Liverpool and Manchester regions into respectively Merseyside and SELNEC (South East Lancashire & North East Cheshire) PTEs, as all of a sudden dozens of Verona green and jonquil buses appeared around the Mersey area whilst SELNEC chose sunglow orange as a base colour. In fact, so proud were they of their work that they even paid for a photo of the first vehicles to carry the livery to appear as one of the first colour covers of *Buses*. It has to be said that the result was quite startling in a drab Victorian city like Manchester, though unfortunately this colour hasn't stood the test of time and has been replaced by steadily deeper shades of orange, to the point that, as the author writes, some buses of GM North have settled for red.

And of the buses themselves, the changes seen in this book speak for themselves. So sad are subsequent developments that I prefer to draw the story to a close before the time that the political hue of the nation went from red to blue, and to remember the happy days as seen through rose-tinted glasses.

* *The Manchester Tram* by Ian Yearsley, published by Oakwood Press, 1962, and reprinted as part of *The Manchester Tramways*, Transport Publishing Co, 1988

Left: This era saw the introduction of the all-over advertising bus and, especially in its early days, there were many quite clever examples like the 'Everton Mint' Atlantean, but for the most colourful example I have chosen this SELNEC ex-Manchester Corporation Mancunian-style Fleetline No 2274 advertising the *Manchester Evening News* and seen in Piccadilly, the city's transport hub.
Howard J. Piltz

Above: Chester sits to the south of the Merseyside conurbation and borders the North Wales region and consequently grew up as a major junction of routes in bygone days, bestowing on the city its rich heritage so beloved of today's tourists. A small tram system was based on the railway station, the tram depot being opposite, but was replaced by buses in 1930. Being the county town of Cheshire it was not altogether surprising that a local chassis manufacturer, in this case Foden, was tried. This was an example of municipal benevolence that we shall see repeated frequently in this book, as it was widespread throughout the country until mischief-makers and cynics ruled it 'politically unacceptable'. No 76 is one of eight with Massey bodies purchased in the 1948–51 period. *Geoff Lumb*

Above: Chester Corporation must have been impressed with its solitary wartime acquisition, a Massey-bodied Guy Arab II. Having sampled most of the popular makes of chassis since scrapping the trams, it did what one or two other operators did (as we shall see later) and the unswerving diet after the Fodens was the Arab IV and later Arab V until the make was no longer available. Waiting alongside the city's cathedral is No 40, a 30ft-long Arab V, not only one of the last of the breed but also noteworthy as an example of Massey bodywork built immediately before that company's take-over by fellow Wigan-based Northern Counties. *Howard J. Piltz*

Above: Crosville also had its head office in Chester, covering the northern half of Wales together with a significant presence north to Liverpool and east into Cheshire. Could the introduction of the Leyland National constitute part of the industry's heyday? Why not? Here we have state-of-the-art technology with a body structure that, as we shall see, has proved particularly long-lived, although the engine might not have been so successful, contributing to the concept of noise pollution. So here we see the second production machine, UFM801K, on its first day in service. Seen at Chester Zoo, it hadn't yet received its fleet number — SNL801 — and very soon after was re-registered WFM801K in line with the rest of

the batch of 24. Together with several others that on withdrawal by Crosville found their way to airside work at London Gatwick Airport, this bus was one of a large number purchased in 1995 at auction by the newly privatised GM Buses South, based at Stockport, who spent a large amount of money rebuilding them for further service. Numbered 265 and still being worked on when the Stagecoach organisation bought GMS in early 1996, it is rather ironic that the first production Leyland National, originally delivered to SELNEC PTE, had by this time been in Manchester's Boyle Street museum for over 10 years!

Howard J. Piltz

Above: Having retraced our steps a little and headed up the Wirral peninsula, we come to Birkenhead, famous for ship building and to students of road transport as the landing point in 1860 for one George Francis Train who brought with him from America the horse tram. Horse buses were here first, whilst electric trams started in 1901 and the motorbus in 1905, the rush being to serve both the local industry and also the Woodside Ferry Terminal for the Mersey crossing to Liverpool's Pier Head. However, here we see something a little more modern: No 172 is a 1949 Daimler CVG6 with Massey body displaying the characteristic body styling of that firm as well as this fleet's most attractive blue and cream livery.
Photobus/Roy Marshall

7

Above: Throughout the 1950s and 1960s Birkenhead's main suppliers of bodywork were East Lancs or Massey. However, in 1954 it turned to Weymann for a batch of Leyland PD2/12s, of which No 258 (CBG 558) was an example, seen in 1965. The Liver Building at Liverpool's Pier Head is visible across the Mersey. *Geoff Lumb*

Right: Looking out into Liverpool Bay and the Irish Sea at the northern tip of the Wirral peninsula is Wallasey, which took advantage of the area's position to become the playground beside the sea for Merseysiders. Public transport came courtesy of Crosville, whose services were usually longer distance, whilst for the local community the service was in the care of Wallasey Corporation. Its history went back to the horse trams operated from 1879 by local entrepreneurs until parliamentary powers of 1899 allowed the corporation to purchase the routes and begin electrification, although trams gave way to motorbuses rather earlier than most, in 1933. In postwar years, the corporation was a committed Leyland user and remained so until absorbed into the Merseyside PTE. Illustrating early postwar deliveries are these PD2s, with bodies by Metro Cammell and Burlingham, both of which carry the beautiful, old-style 'Wallasey Corporation Motors' fleetname. *Geoff Lumb*

Left: Wallasey was one of the first recipients of production Atlanteans; fittingly it first began a new sequence at No 1 in 1958, whilst No 30 was the last of the batch that came in 1961. It clearly shows the lack of creativity in its styling. *Geoff Lumb*

Above: To take a ferry from either Wallasey or Birkenhead across the River Mersey to the great seaport of Liverpool was once an everyday event for hundreds of thousands of people, stepping ashore at the world-renowned Pier Head to find buses of three major operators awaiting their patronage. Today the railway and two road tunnels have all but put the ferries out of business, buses no longer bother going to the Pier Head, and the character of the city has lost incalculable volumes. The city's corporation fleet consisted of smart big buses in a glowing shade of green (if green could be said to glow!) which differentiated them from the Crosville buses that served outlying areas to the south and which tended to be low-height Bristols that always had a well-scrubbed appearance.

Representing some of the older buses around in our era is No A499, a 1947 AEC Regent II. The well-equipped Edge Lane Works had built many of the city's trams and consequently had no difficulty in finishing bodies delivered as basic frames, in this case by Weymann. This bus started out as No A299, and is seen here in later life as a driver trainer on Queens Drive, the city's major ring road at the time, near Townsend Avenue. *Geoff Lumb*

Right: A51 was a Regent III, of 1954, but Crossley only built the frames and the LCT Edge Lane works finished the job off with characteristic Liverpool style, and a 'bull-nose' front. This Regent is seen at Edge Lane Works. *Collection R. Wilson*

Left: 'The style that breathed new life into bus design' is how Liverpool's first production batch of Atlanteans was described after the bland tin boxes seen so far. No L568 illustrates what was, at the time, a startling sight, having just received another 'fad' of the time — the illuminated side advertisement display box. It is seen soon after delivery in July 1963 at Gillmoss depot. *Collection R. Wilson*

Above: It always seemed that every tram and bus heading for the city centre in Liverpool showed the unmistakable destination — 'Pier Head'. Here we see part of the major gyratory area in front of the world-famous riverfront scene. Unfortunately, the batch of Metro Cammell-bodied Leyland Panthers were not as long-lasting as the panorama and went quickly with few regrets. *Geoff Lumb*

Right: With the fall in importance of the Mersey ferries, and following deregulation of local bus services in 1986, buses abandoned Pier Head in favour of the more central area around Roe Street. Today the unfettered competition seems far removed from this almost serene scene in front of the Royal Court Theatre. *Geoff Lumb*

Above: Follow the River Mersey upstream on the A56, cross the river and the Manchester Ship Canal on the Runcorn–Widnes Suspension Bridge then drop down into the chemical town of Widnes. Here a splendid, small fleet of Leyland Titans disported itself in a rich shade of red and deep (almost clotted) cream, as exemplified by No 1, the Leyland-bodied PD1/1, so numbered because it was the fleet's first postwar addition, whilst a later East Lancs-bodied example basks in the reflected glory of St Paul's Church in Victoria Square.
Geoff Lumb

Above: A little further up the Mersey is Warrington, another town that has grown due to its position beside the Manchester Ship Canal where it and the river are crossed by the ex-LMS West Coast main line. Nowadays, of course, the town is also almost surrounded by motorways: the M6 to the east, whilst the M62 and M56 skirt respectively to the north and south. Whether as a result of these, or contributing to their presence, one must also record that in Warrington there is a brewery and a vodka distillery! The local authority bus fleet was founded in 1913, gradually replacing trams that lasted until 1935. Noteworthy were the particularly narrow streets in both the town and outlying areas that required 7ft 6in-wide buses made as recently as 1965, about 15 years after everyone else. Here we see Foden No 36 (not surprisingly, as Foden was based not many miles down the road in Sandbach), but notice the odd fit of the body on this chassis, a clue to the interesting history of this bus. The chassis was the prototype PVD6 model produced in 1945, and with a Willowbrook body became demonstrator HMB 395. The chassis was sold to Warrington in 1948, and received the Metro Cammell body from 1935 Crossley No 30 (ED 8700). *Geoff Lumb*

15

Above: As if to disprove what has been said about patronage of local industry, Warrington Corporation also made the most unlikely choice for its deliveries in 1949/50, going to Bristol for the K5G chassis, and having rare Bruce bodywork fitted. No 69 is a 1950 example. *Photobus/A. Douglas*

Right: To the world, the town of St Helens has long meant glass. Glass for windows as well as all its by-products. The municipality began tramway operation in 1911 and replaced the trams with trolleybuses by 1936, which in turn succumbed to the motorbus by 1958. Representing the fondly remembered red and cream livery is No 2, a Metro Cammell-bodied AEC Regent V of 1961. *Geoff Lumb*

Left: St Helens' No 209 was a rather interesting one-off, being its first underfloor-engined bus — an AEC Regal IV with dual-door Roe bodywork. It was built in 1951 specially to operate between Warrington and Southport, double-deckers being precluded by a low bridge until shortly after No 209 appeared, after which she was relegated to less glamorous work until withdrawal in 1965. *Geoff Lumb*

Above: On the coast to the north of Liverpool is the distinguished seaside resort of Southport. Never the place for 'Kiss-me-Quick' hats or toffee-apples, it is a place where day trippers can enjoy the elegance of Lord Street, spending hours simply browsing along the rows of tempting shops forming a second promenade inland, under virtually continuous glass awnings. Surveying my slides, this view brought back a long-forgotten memory, of the characteristic rear of a postwar Weymann bus body as illustrated by No 21, a 1952-built Titan PD2/12. Some of Lord Street's shops can be glimpsed, obviously on a quiet day here, as can another forgotten sight, the short-lived Ford Corsair.
Howard J. Piltz

Still going north and approaching
Preston, the independent operator
Fishwick's of Leyland was like as not
to be the first sign of the area's local
operators. Individualistic to this day,
the two-tone green livery was
invariably bestowed on the products
of their home town, and so it was in
this depot shot taken in May 1966
(*right*). It is pleasing to note that
preserved representatives of this fleet
include No 5, a Weymann lowbridge-
bodied Titan from the same batch as
No 21 seen here and No 7, a 1957
Leyland Olympian (*below right*). The
latter, a first generation Olympian, is
an integral construction single-decker
built by Weymann with Leyland Tiger
Cub running gear, and from the same
batch as the rather fine coach-seated
machine seen opposite. *Above:
Geoff Lumb. Below: Howard J. Piltz*

Above: Another well-remembered operator entering Preston from the south was Bamber Bridge Motor Services, the trading name of R. Prescott & Son Ltd. Unlike Fishwick's which still flourishes today, this fleet was submerged in the Ribble empire in April 1967. Back in 1954, though, this AEC Regent III with East Lancs bodywork was a Motor Show exhibit for AEC and folk-lore has it that it came north to Leyland's backyard as mischievous provocation by a less than happy operator. It is believed now to be safe in preservation.
Geoff Lumb

Above: The distinguished name of Ribble traces its history back to local operations in the Preston area as far back as 1910, the company being formed as Ribble Motor Services Ltd in 1919. It expanded to become the major provider of bus services in Lancashire as well as in large tracts of the Lake District as far up as Carlisle, either alongside the myriad of municipalities in the county or providing inter-urban and country services. Being based so close to Leyland's manufacturing base, the standard double-decker was, naturally enough, the Titan, and 2756 was a 1950 example with Leyland's own lowbridge bodywork. *Geoff Lumb*

Above: Also close at hand was the bodybuilding firm of Burlingham at Blackpool which was frequently favoured with orders from Ribble. No 1431 was a characteristic example of its work, the more rounded corners to windows being a particular give-away on the 1956-built PD2. Both these Titans illustrate the well-known Ribble hexagonal destination aperture that seems to have been adopted from a small batch of 'unfrozen' Leyland-bodied TD7s diverted from Scotland's W. Alexander & Sons in 1940. The early Atlantean seen here pursuing No 1431 in Burnley's town centre also carries the layout as did other double-deckers until 1967. *Geoff Lumb*

Above: As a child there was always a rising tide of excitement for me on a family trip as we approached Preston for it usually meant we were off on another day out or longer holiday to Blackpool. Preston grew from its position at the lowest crossing point of the River Ribble where a fairly large dock complex grew up. Even today it is easy to see the importance of its position by looking at a map. Britain's first stretch of motorway was the M6 around Preston and today it has become the node between south and southeast routes one way, and those going north, northeast and northwest another way. Apart from the Ribble fleet and the independents already mentioned, local services were predominantly the responsibility of the municipality up until deregulation in 1986. This 1964 view shows one of Preston Corporation's unique in-house conversions: what were rear-entrance, fairly ordinary Leyland-bodied Titan PD2/10s were lengthened and given front entrances, in this case during 1960, to become a PD3/6. The maroon livery did nothing to brighten up this drab scene, but...
Geoff Lumb

Overleaf: ...this one did! 'Once in a Preston Guild' is a quotation taken from the municipal junketing that happens here once every 20 years. In 1972 they painted up a PD3A/1, No 88, to help celebrate the occasion, local employer Dorman Smith sponsoring the job. *Howard J. Piltz*

Above: On the north side of the Ribble estuary we first of all come to that part of the coast so beloved of the elderly: Lytham and St Annes being the places to which one retires. I wonder if in reality these folk prefer the life and sparkle of Blackpool but want to stand back just a few paces! Like the St Annes trams that preceded them, the Lytham St Annes buses enjoyed this splendid and refreshing livery that was such a contrast to the brash neighbour next door. At the entrance to the Squires Gate Lane depot we find tram tracks still in place and a Dakota's tail just visible on Blackpool's airport apron behind, but holding its age well is No 45, a Leyland-bodied Titan TD5c of 1938. This small batch of Titans was particularly interesting, being the final working examples of Leyland's 'Gearless' buses. To assist tramcar drivers to adapt to the complexities of the motorbus, this hydraulic, two-stage 'Torque Converter' transmission was developed by Leyland but fuel consumption suffered terribly and all other late survivors had this arrangement replaced by conventional gearboxes. One cannot help but assume that the full-fronts reflected a perceived need to 'keep up with the Jo… neighbours'.
Geoff Lumb

25

Left: Lytham St Annes No 70, seen here on Blackpool's Promenade with the Tower behind, in a more up-to-date livery style is really little more then a 1964 version of No 45, a little longer and wider but a good example of the longevity of the basic unbreakable Titan formula. Since Leyland had stopped building bodies by then (at least for the time being), Massey did the honours here. *Geoff Lumb*

Above: In a scene redolent of Lytham St Annes gentility is one of the local undertaking's Northern Counties-bodied Leyland Titan PD2/20s of 1957, No 58 (757 CTD). Lytham St Annes almost seemed to make a virtue out of numbering its buses so that they were just one adrift from the registration!
Photobus/A. Douglas

Above: Blackpool is the furthest north our little tour is going, just as it was so often in my youth (oh, so long ago!). To the enthusiast, the town's buses always took second place to the trams but in fact the fleet has a fascinating history with some most attractive vehicle types, virtually all Leylands until accountants got the better of common sense and AEC Swifts started to arrive in 1969. The mainstay of the early postwar fleet were 100 of these locally-built Burlingham centre-entrance Leyland PD2/5 Titans, continuing the prewar style that gave a family link to the famous trams of the era. This is No 224, shown in later years after the livery had been simplified; gone is the green band above the destination display and the friendly 'V', again so reminiscent of the trams. *Photobus/A. Douglas*

Blackpool's single-deckers were equally interesting and here is No 13, a 1940 Tiger TS8 again with Burlingham bodywork. In 1957 it and two others were converted from centre- to forward-entrance for early work on OPO duties whilst (*below*) the similar No 9 had become a Lost Children's Centre on Central Promenade where its appearance was enhanced with a greater area of green paint. *Above: Photobus/A. Douglas. Below: Howard J. Piltz*

Above: Backtrack a little now and follow the northern boundary of the industrial and textile heartland of Lancashire until you see the less flamboyant but none the less attractive livery of Blackburn Corporation's fleet, colours that were carried by the town's enormous-looking trams until 1949. Their replacements were 20 Guy Arab IIIs, rather unusually bodied by Crossley. Nos 132 and 134 are seen in the depot yard. *Geoff Lumb*

Above: Blackburn No 122, another of the unusual and characteristic Crossley-bodied
Guy Arab IIIs, is seen in service close to the city centre.
Photobus/Roy Marshall

Left: Moving on now to a later generation of Guy Arabs in Blackburn, No 164 (NCB 164) is an Arab IV with a 'Johannesburg' style grill, bodied in the town (Blackburn, not Johannesburg!) by East Lancs. Blackburn standardised on these vehicles from 1957, the first time new buses were bought after the 20 Arab IIIs of 1949; No 164 was new in 1961 and still looks spruce a year later. *Geoff Lumb*

Above: Seen in Accrington on a typical inter-urban service is another Guy Arab, this time it's No 152, a Mark IV built in 1958 with an East Lancs body. That this bodybuilder is situated within Blackburn and has fulfilled virtually all this municipality's needs from 1957 until the present day would seem perfectly reasonable to the writer. Also noticeable is yet another fleet that, having tried Guy's at a time of dire necessity, seems to have found their simple ruggedness habit-forming. *Photobus/Roy Marshall*

Above: This splendid Duple Vega Major-bodied Bedford Val 14 of 1963 belonged
to W. Robinson & Sons of Great Harwood, just up the road from Blackburn. Even in
the 1960s one could see the attention to detail that was to establish Robinson's as
one of the premier coach operators of the 1980s and 1990s. *Geoff Lumb*

Above: Head south out of Blackburn towards Bolton and Manchester, and the next town is Darwen where, like life in general, transport has always been closely linked with its larger neighbour to the north. In fact, in the local government reorganisation of 1974, the two were amalgamated. Darwen No 44 predates the amalgamation but illustrates the connection, even if the thought of a double-deck Crossley operating an express service stretches one's imagination a little. The lack of streamline-influenced curves that were a throwback to Manchester's more flamboyant prewar livery, and the full-size rear side windows on both decks, indicate a late true Crossley. She was, in fact, Darwen's last, in 1952, even if 'badge-engineering' saw an AEC Regent and three Reliances carry Crossley badges in this fleet. *Photobus/A. Douglas*

Above: Darwen was one of the very last purchasers of Leyland PD2s; by the time No 37 (ETF 485F) was built, most new front-engined Leylands were PD3s — mostly for municipal operators in the northwest. The East Lancs body shows strong similarities to that on the Blackburn Guy behind, though the rather racy styling for the rear wheelarch was very much a Darwen-ism. It is seen in Blackburn in July 1969; five years later the two undertakings would be amalgamated — and so, to bizarre effect, were their liveries.
Geoff Lumb

Above: Right on the edge of the Pennines in north Lancashire is the compact community that includes the towns of Burnley, Nelson and Colne that amalgamated their various local transport undertakings into the Burnley, Colne & Nelson Joint Transport Committee in April 1933. The Nelson livery of fawn and cream formed the basis of the unusual, if very attractive, livery that survives today under the Burnley & Pendle banner, and these early postwar buses illustrate it for us. Guy Arab II No 140 arrived in 1945 with a Massey utility body as No 22, but was quickly rebodied by East Lancs in 1950 and renumbered in 1956. *Photobus/Roy Marshall*

Above: Like many liveries, variations appeared over the years and often simplification could be attributed to the need of advertisers or a change of painting techniques from brush- to spray-finishing. Here is another Guy Arab II, this time No 66 from 1943. It too started life with a Massey body that was replaced in 1950 but this time by one of the products of Northern Counties. Note the registration prefix letters on these buses — 'HG' — being Burnley's allotted identification letters that adorned all buses purchased new from 1930 (HG298 — a Leyland LT2 purchased by Burnley Corporation) to 1948 (HG 9920 — a Northern Counties-bodied PD2/3 that actually lasted until 1968). *Photobus/Roy Marshall*

Right: And here is one of those 1948 PD2/3s — No 179 (HG 9917). With the position of the three towns on the edge of the Pennines most routes involve a climb out of Burnley. The photographer was later to become the undertaking's general manager. *Photobus/Roy Marshall*

Left: If one is looking for a real off-beat municipal bus livery then look no further than Accrington. In common with a great many other towns in Lancashire, steam trams worked here and were superseded by electric ones that survived until 1932. Being individualistic again, the corporation's liking for Guys culminated in No 157, one of a pair of 1961 Guy Wulfrunians bearing remarkable rear-entrance East Lancs bodies. The Wulfrunian (native of Wolverhampton — home of Guy Motors) was designed, like the later Volvo Ailsa, as a front-engined alternative to the Atlantean and Fleetline whilst retaining the latter's ideal entrance arrangements. Too many innovative engineering features were a fatal flaw in the design and as a result Accrington ended up with the worst of both worlds. *Geoff Lumb*

Right: Drop down from the north through the beautiful valleys of this part of Lancashire and enter the area now known as Rossendale, not the most heavily populated part of the county, but nevertheless served by two municipal operators and in later years even sharing the same General Manager. Haslingden illustrates for us the definitive late prewar corporation bus, a Leyland-bodied Titan TD5, against a backdrop of the typical stone buildings of the area. *Geoff Lumb*

Above: Ramsbottom had no trams but this small Irwell Valley community was very quick to try the trolleybus, from 1913–31. The municipal buses took an early liking to Thornycrofts but thereafter its unswerving diet was Leylands and it was to embrace the final conventional double-decker delivered in Great Britain, the East Lancs-bodied PD3 that was actually delivered to SELNEC as No 6411 when Ramsbottom became the smallest constituent of that undertaking. However, this is an illustration of something earlier: No 7 is a Tiger TS7 with bodywork by East Lancs. *Geoff Lumb*

Above: The particularly bright livery of green and cream always made even the Weymann 'Orion' bodies on Bury Corporation's PD3s stand out as exotic strangers as they entered Manchester along Corporation Street. To a lad from south of the city, Bury was truly a wondrous and strange place! Its trams (the first generation — that is) had run until 1949, when those that didn't find homes afresh were dismantled and used under tons of concrete to fill in the redundant tram pits. No 186 is an earlier PD2 of 1953 that has become SELNEC No 6386 and is seen here in Hyde bus station, where its colour fitted in well working in erstwhile SHMD territory. *Howard J. Piltz*

Above: Bury No 108 was an early Leyland Atlantean of 1963 fitted with a Metro Cammell body to the design used on Liverpool's first batches of Atlanteans. It came as a revelation in both places after the uninspiring designs used on the first rear-engined deckers. *Howard J. Piltz*

Above: As befits a town of such stature, Bolton had the region's largest municipal fleet outside the three cities of Liverpool, Manchester and Salford. In later days, there was a sizeable fleet of larger vehicles as well; from 1958 almost all double-deck deliveries were 30-footers, a good example being No 146, an East Lancs 73-seater Daimler CVG6 of 1960, that also illustrates well the rich crimson and cream livery. *Howard J. Piltz*

Above: By February 1973, when I took this photograph on a town service in Bolton, the influence of SELNEC was being felt and various initiatives and experiments were being pursued to woo the car driver back on to the buses, as can be guessed from the fleet number of this attractive little precursor to today's Dennis Darts and Volvo B6 midibuses. The Seddon Pennine IV was built close-by in Oldham and designed for city centre and lightly-used country routes but, except for the experimental battery-powered example, it didn't endear itself to drivers and passengers alike due to the intrusiveness, mess and noise from the front-mounted engine. *Howard J. Piltz*

Above: Lancashire United Transport was Britain's biggest independent bus operator in the 1950s, operating over 400 buses and coaches and centred on the mining and cotton towns west of Salford and east of St Helens. Headquarters were at Howe Bridge, Atherton, that had previously been home to the trams and trolleybuses of South Lancs Transport, predecessor to LUT. This view is taken at Howe Bridge and apart from No 448, one of five Foden PVD6s bought in 1951, we see No 567, a 1942 Guy Arab I delivered with Roe utility bodywork but rebodied in 1955 by Northern Counties and showing probably the prime example of how the Guy company capitalised on its war work in producing such fine buses in straitened times. From 1942 until 1945 Guy supplied 58 utility buses to LUT and was subsequently rewarded by orders for no less than 316 buses and coaches up until 1967. *Howard J. Piltz*

Right: LUT was never afraid of dealing with several different manufacturers at once; hence every now and then Dennis supplied some chassis, perhaps for old-time's sake, for, bar two very early false starts in 1906 and 1914, the first motor buses for LUT were Dennises, Nos 1–36 of 1919/20. Biding its time within the Atherton depot complex is 196, a 1947 Dennis Lance with characteristic Weymann lowbridge bodywork, and one of 29 chassis to arrive from the Guildford manufacturer that year. Together with another 15 in 1949, they were the only Dennises to come between 1936 and the Lolines of 1959/60. *Geoff Lumb*

Left: It should never be forgotten that LUT also operated a substantial fleet of coaches on a wide spectrum of work. Awaiting incoming passengers at Manchester's Ringway Airport is No 145, a 1963 AEC Reliance with dual-purpose Plaxton Highwayman bodywork. *Howard J. Piltz*

Above: In 1955, LUT's Chairman and Managing Director — E. H. Edwards — retired at the age of 80, and died later that year. Such was his stature that no one man could fulfil his many roles, so to the post of General Manager came C. C. Oakham, recruited from Manchester Corporation Transport Department where he was Chief Engineer, and did it show?! The combination of the prolific MCW 'Orion' bodywork, Manchester destination display layout and the all-pervading red paint made it easy to mistake the identity of a member of the fleet at a glance, but the connoisseur would notice the grey band and the extra length of a 30-footer on a back-loader that Manchester never used. I must have taken this photograph of Guy Arab IV No 43 at Blackpool's Coliseum express coach station on a busy summer Saturday when everything and anything that could run, did run on the famous X60 Manchester–Blackpool service. *Howard J. Piltz*

Above: Mainstay of Salford's fleet during the 1950s and 1960s were 195 virtually identical Metro Cammell-bodied Daimler CVG6s, built between 1950 and 1952, the last few of which survived to join the SELNEC fleet. In this view are two of them turning from Bridge Street into Deansgate, Manchester, illustrating the two principal livery variations of the fleet up to take-over. No 513 shows the original scheme, save that when new the buses were delivered with aluminium roofs, black mudguards and a small red dome between the front upper-deck windows to signify that they were 8ft wide. Even the simplified livery on the bus behind cannot fail to remind us that this fleet had a reputation for smartness and good maintenance absolutely second to none. *Howard J. Piltz*

49

Above: Salford's Victoria Bus Station lurked under the shadow of Manchester's sooty-black cathedral just across the Irwell River that acted as the boundary between the two cities. Turning into that bus station, on the left of the photographer and showing that enigmatic destination is AEC Reliance No 104, one of Salford's few single-deckers that were needed due to a low bridge under the Bridgewater Canal. *Geoff Lumb*

Above: There was another single-decker in the Salford fleet at this time, but one that would not carry the destination 'Victoria', for No 101 was the Transport Committee coach of 1962. When SELNEC took over in 1969 such frivolities were not to be countenanced and a quick respray found it earning its keep on the Airport service (26 seats and all!) where it was photographed lined up with a brand-new Plaxton-bodied Bedford VAL bought by Manchester Corporation specifically for the job. The photographer got a salutary lesson when mileage readings on the two coaches were compared — 9,726 on both! *Howard J. Piltz*

Left: Next to it is the great cotton city of Manchester where our tour continues, where the streets play host to not only the City Transport Department's own fleet of red buses and trolleybuses but also the kaleidoscope of other operators, municipal as well as major and minor company fleets. Naturally, with a fleet close to 1,500 machines, the Manchester bus predominated and whether it was this prewar Daimler COG5 with Metro Cammell-framed Crossley bodywork (renumbered from 1257), or any other of the M.C.T.D. buses illustrated in this book, they all possessed a certain lineage that stamped them as 'Manchester'.
F. P. Roberts

Above: The large city fleets have the benefit of size to be able to afford extensive engineering facilities to back up operations and for Manchester the principal facility was at Hyde Road, Ardwick, together with a large yard at Bennett Street that was separated from the Hyde Road Works by the elevated tracks of the railway line into London Road (now Piccadilly) Station. Seen at Bennett Street and looking more like a motorised bath-tub is this Bristol 4-tonner of 1924. Converted from a front-entrance single-decker into general purpose lorry No A80 in 1930, it is quoted in *The Manchester Bus* (Michael Eyre and Chris Heaps, Transport Publishing Co, 1989) as having been sold for preservation in 1963. Where is it now? *Geoff Lumb*

Above: Also seen at Bennett Street, in 1966, are some of the many dozens of redundant buses and trolleybuses that were ranked up here awaiting their fate following another influx of what were regular deliveries of new buses for fleet renewal. Whilst MCTD maintained a policy of dual-sourcing up until SELNEC days, the exigencies following the aftermath of war and the need to finally rid the city of tramcars in 1949 dictated three suppliers would be favoured with orders until the final Crossley Dominion trolleybus was delivered late in 1951. This scene shows Leylands, Daimlers and Crossleys, some already robbed for spares before going for scrap. *Howard J. Piltz*

Above: The archetypal Manchester motorbus of the postwar era has to be the standard
8ft wide Manchester-specified streamlined body that went onto 598 chassis. In the author's view
the most handsome were the Leyland PD1/3 and PD2/3s with Metro Cammell bodywork like
PD1/3 No 3195 seen here cruising through an uncannily quiet Piccadilly. *Howard J. Piltz*

Above: Back to Bennett Street again, to an open day SELNEC held in April 1973 where, using an ex-Manchester PD2, instructors demonstrated their prowess on the skid pan that survives into the 1990s as the only one left in the bus industry. I have to confess that this is the only picture I have taken of a moving bus with daylight showing under a wheel! *Howard J. Piltz*

Above: From 1964 to 1966 Manchester standardised on MCW-bodied Daimler Fleetlines and Leyland Atlantean PDR1/2s. One of the 1966 deliveries, Fleetline No 4737 (FNE 737D), stands in Piccadilly bus station — which was replaced by a row of bus shelters and a turning circle in 1996 — in the evening peak probably in winter 1970/71, waiting to leave for Firswood on a 66x — or maybe just a 66,

'x's were often used indiscriminately. Although little seems to have changed — a Salford Atlantean loads on the stand behind, where Salford Atlanteans did for several years on the 15 to Worsley — the sharp-eyed may just detect a Manchester-style fleetnumber on the Salford bus while on the other side of the shelter an orange-painted Mancunian betrays the fact we are now into the SELNEC era. *Howard J. Piltz*

57

Above: As bus rides go, a journey from central Manchester to Rochdale would be fascinating if it were in this 1948 AEC Regent III with 7ft 6in-wide Weymann bodywork, a trip I did several times after I left school, as a young lad travelling around for my first boss and exploring my new-found world. Apart from the never-to-be-forgotten music of the AEC, much of Lancashire life was out there to see, from cotton mills to the myriad of other industries that made up the economy of the region, regrettably much of it now gone for ever — as has No 44. Much the same has to be said of when the journey was over, for Rochdale was the birthplace of the Co-operative movement and of course of 'our Gracie', the well-remembered singer Gracie Fields who will forever be synonymous with the town. Somehow, when the elegantly flowing lines on corporation buses were replaced, the town lost a little bit of itself. *Geoff Lumb*

Above: After having a fleet consisting almost exclusively of AECs, Rochdale turned to the Daimler Fleetline in 1964 for its next generation of buses. Whilst the simplification of the livery wasn't appreciated by all, there is little denying its suitability on this distinguished-looking tin box, the fluted Daimler badge being almost out of place. Having adopted SELNEC fleet No 6241, this 1969 example is seen in Bury turning into the Haymarket close to what today is the Bury Interchange on the route jointly operated with Bury Corporation between the two towns. *Howard J. Piltz*

Above: No review of buses in the northwest would be complete without mention of
Yelloways. From a side street in central Rochdale Yelloways ran a thriving
independent express coach service renowned for its thoroughbred AEC Reliances,
until big business bought the company after the close of our era, found it didn't
understand the first thing about the subject and shut it down as a dead loss, hanging its
head in shame in the process. In happier days, these two early Reliances with
Burlingham Seagull coachwork show one of Yelloways individualistic features, side
destination boxes with doubtless sufficient towns to fill an A-Z of Britain. *Geoff Lumb*

Another independent coach operator based in Rochdale was Ellen Smith (Tours) Ltd, and happily still flourishing today, if now in the hands of Rossendale Transport. This operator had a habit of sniffing out the something special, and this is the second of two Leyland Royal Tiger Worldmasters bodied by Plaxton, one in 1956, and this one in 1958 (*right*). This principally export chassis had been developed in the mid-1950s for the most extreme motoring conditions and did so well for Ellen Smith's that both were rebodied by Plaxtons in 1970 (*above*) and are believed to survive in preservation today. *Howard J. Piltz/John Burgoyne Collection*

Above: Going south, Oldham is another mill town on the very edge of the Pennines, with yet another proud municipal fleet of buses. Trams worked here from 1900 until 1946 and bequeathed to their successors the smart livery of maroon and white that even retained its complicated lining-out until quite late in the day. Roe and Leyland were the preferred suppliers if not to the exclusion of others, No 228 being an example of that combination, and was the first of 64 PD1s supplied between 1946–8. *Geoff Lumb*

Above: A later shade of maroon was used in the 1960s, described as 'pommard' and it can be seen here on No 420, a 1958 Metro Cammell-bodied Titan PD2/30 with the preserved Crossley DD42/8 No 368 for comparison. No 420 was about to set out on the service 59 from its unusual terminal on Manchester's Piccadilly Station approach, where the Crossley has been pulled up for a photo opportunity. The Ian Allan bookshop is today sited directly behind where I stood to take this photograph. *Howard J. Piltz*

*Above:*Ashton-under-Lyne had a small corporation fleet that had included trolleybuses from the days of the solid tyre right through to 1966, and it was in its Mossley Road depot that I learned of the pride with which some fleets were maintained. Ne'er a dented panel, even an unpainted one, would be allowed through those depot doors; after all, a keen bodyman could change a panel in less time than it takes to pen these notes and you'd be amazed what tricks were used to get paint to dry. Behind the depot in SELNEC days and parked up at the end of its road is No 66, a 1956 Guy Arab IV with rare S. H. Bond bodywork. Bond was based in Wythenshawe, south of Manchester, and was but a brief presence in the bus body field. Apart from these four Arab IVs, Ashton received eight bodies on new BUT trolleybuses and two more used to rebody wartime ones.
Howard J. Piltz

Above: Ashton standardised on the workmanlike Roe-bodied PD2 for several batches in the early 1960s, and seen here is one such in Stockport's Mersey Square after SELNEC had made its mark. Even in 1963, when No 33 was new, the cherished registration number caused operators some problems, and had No.33 been allocated a registration in line with the rest of this batch it would have been 333 TF. *Howard J. Piltz*

Left: SHMD, the grandly titled Stalybridge, Hyde, Mossley & Dukinfield Joint Tramways & Electricity Board, was formed by Act of Parliament in 1900 and began operating (with a tram borrowed from Ashton-under-Lyne) in 1903; in fact, had a last-minute disagreement not intervened, Ashton would have made it a club of five. This area is more rural than most we have visited on our tour, embracing areas well into the Pennines and hence financial equilibrium was always a struggle. Motorbuses, first used in 1925, were all Thornycrofts until Daimlers became the preferred type in 1936, providing the bulk of the chassis until absorption by SELNEC. No 48 is an East Lancs-bodied Daimler CVD6 and could well be

illustrating the behaviour of the author in his youth. Thank heaven for platform doors! *Geoff Lumb*

Above: The well-known stabling point at the Joint Board's Tame Street, Dukinfield depot had special arrangements to avoid damage due to freezing temperatures. These little boxes housed electrical connections to heating elements fitted into each bus's cooling system. Next to the Atkinson Alpha 109 is the sole Daimler Freeline in the fleet, No 105 (renumbered from 67), and by this time withdrawn. *Howard J. Piltz*

67

Above: Such was the individualism maintained by many bus operators that as a youngster I often imagined how a bus from one fleet would look in the livery of another. To me, SHMD owned the rounded, softer bodies of Northern Counties mounted on sophisticated Daimler chassis with semi-automatic gearboxes, but had no place in the fleet for the utilitarian Stockport brand of buses that were worlds apart, like the early Leyland PD2 with crash gearboxes and altogether more severe Leyland body. So one of the bigger surprises in the earlier days of the SELNEC take-over was the painting of an ex-Stockport Corporation PD2 into SHMD's green livery with gilt fleet numbers in the SHMD series, to boot. Apparently Stockport

had several redundant PD2s still maintained in exemplary order whilst the erstwhile SHMD fleet was short of capacity. Here we see the shocking result: what had been Stockport's No 298 was now No 52, but what must have been an excess of green paint in the stores obviously didn't extend to the second example, on the left, as No 51. The same thing happened to another of Stockport's PD2s at Oldham and to confuse the issue this one initially received a SELNEC fleet number in the series set aside for ex-Oldham buses. It didn't look out of place though, as Oldham already had some indigenous all-Leyland PD1s, and had acquired others from Halifax and Bolton, second-hand. *Geoff Lumb*

Above: As illustrated in the previous picture, the Stockport Corporation fleet was always maintained in first-class order, and the elderly buses seen here looked fit for many years' service instead of being ready for retirement when photographed on an enthusiasts' tour. On the right is No 188, a centre-entrance, English Electric-bodied prewar Leyland Tiger TS7, whilst in the centre is No 217, a wartime Massey utility-bodied Guy Arab II of 1944. To the author's abiding regret, he didn't have his camera with him on the day the final four of these buses were lined up outside their Mersey Square depot, each displaying trade plates, as if getting a civic farewell before starting their journeys to the knacker's yard.

F. P. Roberts

Above: Typifying the Stockport fleet of the late 1940s/early 1950s are its two standard types of the era. Both have bodywork by the chassis builder; standing outside the Corporation's Mersey Square depot, on service, is a 1951 all-Leyland Titan PD2/1, No 306 (EDB 560), one of 44 similar buses, some delivered in 1949, the rest in 1951, and just inside the depot entrance is 1948 all-Crossley DD42/5 No 254 (CJA 778), which would have been built in the town. The former 'Tramway' depot has rather clumsily been altered to a 'Transport' depot, following the abandonment of the trams in 1951 — the last in the Manchester area. *Geoff Lumb*

Above: Also based in Stockport is the original North Western Road Car Company, the BET subsidiary that can trace its history back to the British Automobile Traction Co that commenced operations in this region in Macclesfield in 1913. It expanded after World War 1 into Buxton in 1920 and finally setting up home in Stockport the year after. Its well-known name was adopted in 1923 after which the company grew relentlessly into one of the region's major operators, with its buses and coaches a familiar sight throughout the UK. Possibly no better representative of this fondly remembered fleet is this preserved 1936 Leyland TS7 Tiger that was delivered with a Harrington coach body but suffered like a great many in the fleet from body-swapping until it received its final body, shown here by Windover in 1950. It entered preservation in 1957.

Howard J. Piltz

Above: North Western had retained a predilection for Bristols from the first deliveries in 1936 through the famine caused at nationalisation as part of the 'Tilling' group, and into the era when British Leyland had taken a shareholding and released the marque back on to the open market in 1968 when North Western was to be found clamouring at the door of the Bristol works. A long series of REs culminated in the batch of RELL6Ls with standard ECW bodywork that commenced with fleet No 382. No 388 is believed to be the last one delivered to North Western, whilst I think No 389 seen here went directly into Crosville ownership when the fleet was dispersed to surrounding operators when SELNEC took over services in the Greater Manchester area. The paper 'On Hire' sticker in the front windscreen indicated the days immediately after the transfer but when the route licences had not yet been reissued. This batch was repainted in Crosville's green so quickly it is reputed that the paint applied by ECW so recently was barely dry, and hence photos of these buses in this livery are rare. *Howard J. Piltz*

Above: Before its final demise, North Western's orders for Bristols were further developed with a batch of 25 of the VR double-decker that, like the REs just mentioned, were specified with standard ECW bodywork, and doubtless under different circumstances their numbers would have grown significantly. They finally arrived into a different world as part of the SELNEC Cheshire company set up to encompass the elements of North Western taken over by SELNEC, bearing the fleet numbers 400–24 (but later to become Nos 1400–24), orange paint and Manchester-style destination displays, but notice their 'via' blind was painted out! Like other vehicles transferred to the erstwhile Stockport depots, management had much trouble persuading platform staff to take on the responsibility for additional destination blinds. Nos 407 and 424 are seen on the rough ground behind Mersey Square that for many years was the lay-over point for North Western buses and is now the site of the town's bus station, still with the backdrop of the famous brick arches of the railway's main line viaduct. *Howard J. Piltz*

Left: Close-by Stockport is the market town of Altrincham illustrated in an earlier scene, and was also the home of the Jackson Shearings Pleasureways Ribblesdale group, the well-known coach tour operator that in subsequent years was to become one of the forerunners of today's Shearings organisation. The Ribblesdale element consisted of the tour licences (in the days of high regulation when licences were your most valuable stock-in-trade) and a small number of coaches acquired in the early 1970s from the Blackburn-based company that interestingly survives today as the legal entity better known as Robinson's of Great Harwood (qv). The acquired coaches were rapidly painted into group livery and put to work. This is the new owner's No 3, a Duple-bodied Bedford VAM5 seen on tour in the beautiful Cheddar Gorge. *Howard J. Piltz*

Right: This 1964 AEC Reliance with Plaxton Panorama bodywork worked all its life based in the northwest. Bought new by A. Mayne & Son Ltd, it passed to Stanway of Crumpsall, Manchester, in late 1971. Stan Pochin cherished this coach until purchased by the author's company — Town & Country Coachways Ltd — in 1977. Based in Wilmslow, Cheshire, this venerable coach then set out on its toughest work so far, travelling to Europe and venturing as far as Luxembourg. Following closure of Town & Country, 'VU' was last heard of as a mobile café in the Merseyside area in 1983. *Howard J. Piltz*

Above: Macclesfield is another market town deep in the heart of agricultural Cheshire and is well known for its silk industry, and to us as the place where North Western's foundations were laid. The thriving network of town and rural services passed to Crosville on the former's break-up, which quickly substituted its own livery on everything red. Seen here entering the bus station adjacent to the depot is what was North Western's No 700 but now renumbered STL905, a 1957 Tiger Cub with Weymann bodywork. Londoners who read this should not be overly concerned; the initials in this fleet number refer to Single deck, Tiger chassis, and Leyland engine (!) a system perpetuated to this day by PMT just down the road from here. Again a rear view well remembered but rarely photographed. (No inference on the author's er ... personal preferences should be made by this comment!)
Howard J. Piltz

Above: Heading back towards our starting point at Chester, the traveller might well pass through Congleton where by chance the casual enthusiast might happen upon this unlikely coach hidden behind one of the local hostelries, the Grove Inn. It is a Plaxton-bodied, rear-engined Foden PVRF6 proudly displaying the title of its owners, the Foden Motor Works Band. *Howard J. Piltz*

Above: Stockport's Heaton Lane depot was replaced by a new one in Daw Bank by SELNEC PTE. The PTE's drive for modernisation was somewhat hampered by Stockport's conservative fleet policy, which had seen Leyland PD2s and PD3s entering the fleet up to the end — indeed only the last handful boasted anything so *avant-garde* as a forward entrance. Admittedly an attempt to move into the modern era was thwarted when an entire batch of Bristol VRTs in build for Stockport was destroyed by fire at the East Lancs factory. The old guard is represented by No 5808 (YDB 8), formerly Stockport No 8, an East Lancs-bodied Leyland PD2A/30 of 1963 (the later ones looked more dated by their use of exposed radiators), to the left of the picture, while to the right a thoroughly modern SELNEC standard Park Royal-bodied Leyland Atlantean AN68 is flanked by two PDR1/2 Atlanteans drafted in from Manchester to facilitate one-person operation. In the middle is perhaps something even more alien to Stockport Corporation, if not to the town itself — No 120 (AJA 120B) is an ex-North Western Park Royal-bodied AEC Renown. The date is April 1974.

Howard J. Piltz

Above: Definitely right off the end of our tour of the northwest is London's Victoria Coach Station. But the northwest interest is there, alongside the United Counties Bristol RELH recently out-shopped in clinical National Express white. W. C. Standerwick of Blackpool was finally taken over by Ribble in 1935 and continued as a coaching subsidiary. From the opening of the M1, Standerwick used new double-deck coaches on the Lancashire-London services, starting in 1959 with 'Gay Hostess' Leyland Atlanteans, when such a name could be used without eyebrows twitching, followed later by the equally impressive, if less reliable, ECW-bodied Bristol VRLLHs, the first of which — No 50 (FCK 450G) — is seen here. *Howard J. Piltz*

The 'Heyday' series from **IAN ALLAN** *Publishing*